And Freddie
Was My Darling

CB FOLLETT

Many Voices Press
Flathead Valley Community College

ISBN 978-0-9795185-2-2
Library of Congress Control Number: 2008937055
Library of Congress Cataloging in Publication Data
1. Poetry 2. Follett, CB -- Poetry 3. United States -- 21st Century -- Poetry

Book design by Jeremy Thornton, www.jftdesign.com

Front and back jacket art © by CB Follett, http://members.aol.com/Runes/

Photos from the family album © CB Follett

Many Voices Press
Flathead Valley Community College

777 Grandview Drive
Kalispell, Montana 59901
406 756-3822
ljaeger@fvcc.edu.
www.fvcc.edu/news-events/academic-news/many-voices-press

To Lee, who has been
my Freddie
for over fifty years,
with love.

ACKNOWLEDGEMENTS

JOURNALS

BUFFALO BONES: *If I'd Walked to School*

CADENCE OF HOOVES: A CELEBRATION OF HORSES: *Girls and Horses*

CQ: CALIFORNIA STATE POETRY SOCIETY, First Runner Up: *Baseball*

GOLDEN APPLE PRESS To Climb a Purple Mountain: *Polio*

MEMOIRJOURNAL (and): *Danny*

NORTHWOODS JOURNAL: First Prize: *Women Brushing Hair*

NORTHWOODS JOURNAL: *Some Knowledge of Water Shared*

NOSTALGIA: *War Effort*

PENNINE PLATFORM (England): *The Cow, The Moon, A Glass of Milk*

PLOUGHSHARES: *Leather Boys*

PROCREATION: *Parallel Lives*

PSYCHOPOETICA, Remembering and Forgetting (England): *Where Are My Men*

RUNES, A REVIEW OF POETRY: *The Sap of Spring*

SARASOTA REVIEW: *Copperhead*

SHARP PENCIL: *Final Worries*

SOUTH COAST POETRY JOURNAL: *And Freddie Was My Darling*

THE BRIDGE: *Viewpoint*

THE HELMSMAN: *The Tipsy Dance of Black Can and Red Nun*

THE MACGUFFIN Special Issue – Short Shorts: *Watermelon*

THE MACGUFFIN: *The Day My Uncle Dies*

THE SWEET ANNIE & SWEET PEA REVIEW, Eclectic Woman:
Mary Isabel Sits in Her Room Looking Down on the Street, Religion in a Seed, My Grandmother's Kitchen.

VERVE: *Powder Puff*

WEB DE SOL (online): *Annie's Room*

WHISPERING CAMPAIGN: *Steel Rings*

WITHOUT HALOS: *Chestnut Tree on Forest Street*

ANTHOLOGIES

Gifts Of The Fathers: Heartfelt Remembrances of Fathers and Grandfathers:
War Gone, The Tower Room, Not Here

Marin Poetry Center Anthology – 2005: *The Cow, The Moon, A Glass of Milk*

Ribbet: Of Frogs And Toads: *Longest Leap Outside Calaveras*

Tree Stories: *Hidden Up*

Women And Death: *Not Here*

A few of these poems have appeared in previous collections
in this or different forms. They are included here because
of their relevance to the theme of this book.

I'd like to thank those who have been there in friendship and in poetry: Susan Terris, David St. John, Jeremy Thornton, The Stray Poets, The Cloud View Poets, The Marin Poetry Center, and Joan Sadler, who comes to all the readings.

I thank, as always, my family, who more or less understand my poems and the impulses that birthed them.

And with special thanks to the class of 1954 with whom I shared these years and the memories that turned into poems.

In deference to my family, please keep in mind that the "I" of the poem is not necessarily the "I" of the poet.

CB FOLLETT'S POETRY COLLECTIONS

BOOKS

Hold and Release

At the Turning of the Light *(National Poetry Book Award Winner)*

Visible Bones

Gathering the Mountains

The Latitudes of Their Going

CHAPBOOKS

Poems to Red Rock

A Cat Who Falls From A Tree Branch

Will Always Claim He Meant To

Runaway Girl

The Loving of Trees

CB Follett's Greatest Hits

Bull Kelp

Wheels

Duxbury Reef

Hermit Crab

Arms

Vallon Pont D'Arc

Nightmare Fish

For more information on CB Follett's poetry and art:
http://members.aol.com/runes

TABLE OF CONTENTS

And Freddie
Was My Darling

And Freddie Was My Darling

I

Our first kiss in the cloakroom
among galoshes and stained lunch bags,
hurried pecks, full of blush but no juice.
And in first grade, he keeps me faithful
with a carton of pepsin Chiclets.

Through years of shifting alliance,
we pull each other in tandem.
We have no fathers,
and are solemn about it.
We have no money, and don't care.

In sixth grade, on a movie date,
my mother looming in the front seat
like something Wagnerian,
he gives me five gallons of pollywogs,
in varying stages of semi-frogdom.
They have to be detoured
to my aunt's fishpond, where later,
they ripen into darting greenness
and choke out the pond life.

II

In junior high we cling in Devie's basement,
our socks polish the oaken floor
as we sway to *Slow Boat to China*
and tempt fate again and again.
Here, at last, are the juices.

Close air, and humid. Close dancing.
Swaying bodies and fingers that wander,
Freddie's hand between my legs.
I want that sweet ache to never end,
no matter what my mother says.
I press against him,
murmuring no, put my hand on his,
slowly ease it north, linger
against the tight bulge of his pants,
want what I couldn't want,
what I didn't know,
push off with regret
from his body, from his hot cheek.
His eyes glint,
urging in the near darkness.

III

In high school, proms with crepe streamers
leave blue marks against our sweaty faces
and car windows steam on Bump-Along Lane
where hands know the geography,
kisses are wetter,
though still locked in fear.

And so, we begin to swing in and out of orbit
as Freddie discovers Norwalk
where other girls live, girls
who put out; where boys go
to relieve their aches.

There are a few last beach parties,
but the dark sand is hotter
than our uncertainties,
and the cordite of betrayal stains the air.
By the time we graduate,
we have drifted beyond the heat
of our own hands and hungry mouths,
far beyond the road stretching to Norwalk.

SLIDE SHOW I

For when I remember my grandmother's house on Forest Street and the long shadows of afternoon that slanted across a yard of daffodils, and the huge horse chestnut out my bedroom window that I later climbed looking for sky, then I remember morning glories, and summer thunderstorms, my mother and grandmother and schoolmates and sailboats, sock hops and canteens, holidays and everydays, a snow-covered hill for my small sled, and a black and tan dog willing to follow.

Photo of My Uncle and Me

Tall, burly, wearing a brown suit,
and stuck in his mouth,
in the face that looks like my grandmother's,
one of the cigarettes that will kill him.

He is bent in two and his arms
stretch toward me
squatting considering a daffodil,
so it's spring. The air is soft.

I am lightly dressed,
even my head
for little hair has grown,
a problem for my mother

who wants me to look
like what I am, tired of explaining.
My uncle's hands reach out.
There is a moment of calm

caught by the camera
before he will swoop me up
from the grass and raise me
over his head, and I will squeal

with fear and joy,
high above his head,
smoke from his clenched cigarette
wafting past into the ether.

The Cow, The Moon, A Glass of Milk

When the cow jumped over the moon,
I looked up at my grandmother. *Cows can't*
jump like that, I said, *can they, Grammy?*

Only this cow, she said turning the page. But later
I went outside, the grass damp and deep on my feet
and stared at the moon fattening each night
on the milk of stars. I watched
for the shadow of the cow.

There would be no dish or spoon. I knew
better than that, but a cow might need
to reach the milk-filled moon, like the station
where we got gas, tearing off our ration stamps.
Did the cow, I wondered, need stamps
to fill her udder from the moon tanks?

At bedtime, I always asked for that rhyme.
We might go on to the jerky boy who jumped
over flaming candlesticks, or Jack,
who played with his food, silly
and so like boys, but the cow's magic

held possibilities, as she gracefully levitated
over the peaked roof of my house, above
the sleeping village, and set sail for the moon
rising through the chestnut branches.

If she jumped now, straight up, she might
intercept the moon by midnight, and leap
down again to her clover-sweet meadow
before the stir of sun.

My grandmother was matter-of-fact
and not much given to flights of fancy,
but she willingly poured a glass of milk
that frothed at the lip, extracted slowly
a cookie or two from the jar
kept out of my reach. I would sit

on her warm lap in her warm kitchen,
knowing where the milk came from,
look out at the moon and nod to myself.

Danny

I wasn't much for dolls, too predictable,
but there was Danny,
with his hard rubber head and soft rubbery arms
and legs I could pinch into little peaks
and know it hurt him.

His body was stuffed cloth, and naked.
He was unplucked looking.
So he was always dressed, the same striped shirt
and blue overalls because I wasn't much interested
in bending his arms backward in and out of sleeves
and his toes, little rubber corn kernels,
always snagged on the pant legs. So there was
Danny, complete as he came.

I wanted no one to see that he reduced to
cloth in the middle and in the back
was the hard cylinder of his mama mama
that sounded when you bent him over,
mama mama, a whiny noise
much better when it got clogged somehow
and became deep and slow *Maahw, Maahw.*

Danny improved with age. His hard reddish curls
turned brown with grime and one day
his eyelids that closed so peacefully, thick stiff
lashes lying against his skin, snapped open
for the last time and his honest blue eyes
rolled up into his head and stayed there, only
a small crescent of blue showing at the top,
the rest white and zombie-like.

With his infirmity, Danny came into his own.
Mother and Grandmother were aghast. They tried
to hide him but I searched relentlessly.

They'd beg me to leave him home, which made
him more endearing to me. He was always
with me, tilted downward under my arm
his eyes blank and addled. He would
sit beside me on the couch when old Mrs. Finch
came to call, would ride in the car to Aunt Catherine's
who gave me another doll in hope.

In time, Danny's arms gave up their youthful
springiness and took on the dryness of age,
serious disease overtook his complexion, and his skin
began to separate and fissure. The acne was
overlooked, the skin bandaged until
his limbs looked like lattice, but one fateful day
his left eye gave a metallic gurgle
and fell out, and I, losing patience
at last, gave him up.

Underground, In the Basement

Rubble rubble went the shirts
against the ribbed board, slosh into water,
rubbed again – the enemy grime stalked
through every crease, every congregation of wrinkles.

Rubble down the washboard my grandmother used
in the doghair dust of the basement
while sun slanted through the high window
and suncats danced their reflections in the clothes tub.

In the basement the furnace bellowed
its winter anger, and the room filled with anthracite
shuckled and *chinked*
as it adjusted its facets and corners.

In time to the rhythm of elbows and strong upper arms,
I danced in slow, thoughtless turns
around the concrete floor – saluting
cartons to the south, coal to the east,
north, with its amber cans of peaches
and red tomatoes hunched in mason jars,

and to the west, my grandmother's white hair
in a fireball of sun, flared as she worked
without a sound of her own, only the odd
creaking of wooden board and wooden wringer
and the straining groan of the iron handle turning.

And the soft shoe sounds of my feet dancing –
methodical dervish – one hand up to the sky,
one palm down toward earth; and my grandmother
looking at the wringer; me looking at her
ears, eyes, her tight mouth –
and the parts of her hidden by clothes.

Powder Puff

The powder puffs are out there
and they are not permanent.

Last month, thistles brimmed with bold,
bluer-than-sky tuffets of flowers,
cool against the hot yellow of the meadow.

Now, a few weeks of August have turned them
into a blinding white spume of seedlings,
each with its parasol of flight,

but at this moment, they are powder puffs
for summer girls with scuffed knees and
draggled pinafores.

With my girl scout knife, silver shield
on one side, I cut carefully through the stalk,
the seed-head bigger than my palm. I brush

my cheek with it, my nose, across my closed eyes.
I brush my neck, arms and finally
the shapeless blank of my chest bones

as I have seen my grandmother, with a wink at me,
dust powder on the cleavage of her mysteries.

Mud Flats, Pinchers and a Yellow Ladder

It seems the wrong way to achieve weightlessness
and yet I must learn. Part of the rules
for water freedom: float, tread, swim
to the blue raft

anchored to a bottom far away and deep.
I watch it from shore,
seductive, back-lit into shadow. So small,
and yet a solid thing on star-dappled water.

I can't float anymore than the flat stones
I throw sidearm
and make them skip: two, five, sixteen
until the skips become a slide

breaking stars into a comet's tail
and heading toward the raft but failing,
each stone slides beneath the surface,
water closing over its path as I know

it will claim me,
add my water weight to its own volume.
So I practice swimming
horizontal to the beach, puffing as if each gasp

will move me farther, salt water
stinging the mosquito bites on my legs.
If I can swim, if my arms can find
a rhythm with my legs, if I learn

to tread water, maybe floating will be overlooked.
My neck aches from keeping my face up.
If I look toward bottom, I know
the pinching things are lurking,

their feathery antennae,
their poppy eyes,
silt working over them
like a dirty mop, and when I tire

low-tide mud is even now below me
waiting to coat my legs like knee socks.
To get to the blue float,
I have to make peace with mud

and muscle shells, things that scuttle, slimy things
that laze against rocks sharp
with determined barnacles.
All this I have to cross

to get to water deep enough,
and if I tire, all this is waiting
for my sinking feet, between sand and raft
and the safe hold of the yellow ladder.

First Kiss

We kissed early, hardly out of the womb, it seemed.
I found Freddie and he me, in kindergarten
and we'd kiss in the cloakroom, little rye-krisp kisses,
We'd pucker and peck and be in love forevermore.

Our desks next to each other across the aisle
and our young legs walked them, inched them, closer,
until our heads nearly touched, the heat from our cheeks
bridging the gap.

It was an easy love, too young to argue,
glad to see each other Mondays, but leaving easy
Fridays, knowing there would be another Monday.

On my birthday he gave me, not one, not a package
but a whole box of pepsin Chicklets – clever,
thoughtful boy. None of my family would have
considered it. He won my heart forever,

that and the dimple in his chin, so deep
it sucked in light like a black hole,
and then, it sucked in me.

Not Here

I first noticed
he was needed, in first grade,
when we had to add parents' names
to the accident form.
Please, Miss Carson, I have no father.

Just write deceased, dear. And she turns
to chalk it on the board.
(No one got divorced then.)
You too, Freddie, she says to my love,
giver of pepsin Chiclets.

Freddie cries for his dead soldier father
and blurs his page.
Our glances meet in mutual loss,
in shame at being different,
in pride at being different.

Mother and Grandmother try to tell me
I look pretty, but theirs is not
the backboard I need to hit against.
In junior high, I have no sleeves
to roll in perfect flat folds,
no long curved tails to hang outside my jeans.

In college, Fathers' Weekend,
a Spencer Tracy-Elizabeth Taylor event.
Softball, hikes, a Saturday night dance
to celebrate genetic linkage.
All those fond fathers and daughters.

My non-genetic uncle comes and I love him
for doing so, filling in as best he can
with the necessary proud looks.

That same dear uncle walks me
down the aisle, pressures my arm
with confidence. Stands in an empty place
and tries to overshadow for me,
that ghostly absence.

Copperhead

Often I remember copperheads
and the woods: this seems enough.

How we walked deep into autumn,
the air full of falling,

under a copperhead sun, hot and still,
warming the outcrops into sun ledges

where creatures with cold blood
draw in enough warmth to get through the night.

The river had succeeded through summer
full and urgent. Somewhere a squirrel chittered.

I never, really, saw the man.

Somewhere in her body, my mother sensed his nearness,
turned and saw him exposed,

his penis rising like a saprophyte from the loam of his fly
or so I imagine it now. Suddenly, I felt

her firm grip on my arm and was yanked into the air.
Is it possible, as I remember, that I was hauled

horizontal as a streamer back along the path;
my mother running full out, shoving me into the car,

me panting, *but I want to see, I didn't see,*
looking out as the tires kicked up a jitterbug of gravel,

hoping to catch a glimpse of the man in the woods,
the wild rejected offering he made to us.

Cobb's Hill

I am at the top of the hill, standing
slack-legged, with Libby and Isabel. We
are towheaded into whiteness
and slim as sticks, except Isabel,
whose striped shirt is wavy over her round tummy.

At the top of the hill we look down
on an ocean wave of green. This is our
rolling hill, but we are uncertain at beginnings.
Spread out spread out so we don't bang.
We are Jill watching Jack tumble and crack,
his pail careening after him – all bounce and bruise.
Libby goes first, Issy will always be last
and not go straight. I lay myself full length
on the lush, late-spring grass, tip my nose
into its crushed scent, play my hands over it
gauging thickness, roll over to the sky, and slowly,
tilting like a log ready to go, I slide off
the lip of the hill and begin to roll – grass sky grass sky –
prickles tease my elbows and knees,
my hips easy over, my face collecting blades of green,
the grass and sky a blur of aqua,
my mind whip-lashed and crazed.

★

From a branch high in the white oak, I look
down on three stick figures tossed at the hill-bottom,
willy-nilly, dazed, bruised and ridiculously euphoric.
I see the rough passage and the sound of each voice,
and I remember, remembered all the days
that Isabel was the one who rolled through dog doo,
always Isabel, every hill, a fat patch of it
up her back. Her face pink and blotched with
rigor and sweat. Her full lips trembling with humiliation
and the awful badge of brown she will wear the rest
of the day and on into our memories.

Just Playing

Everything I learned early
came from animals.

In woods, the deer played
leapfrog without the vault, pigs
grunted and squealed, cats announced
in the early morning of the night.

Out in the fields,
the most astonishing trunks
hung from horses patient as statues.

There was no one to ask about amazing things.
For my mother they didn't exist.

How could she see only bucolic meadows
and not the raw stamp of sex? I know
she saw the dogs, their determined
forward dance and the mount,

just playing, she'd say and try to divert
my attention to the safety of flowers,

but I had seen enough
to know that if it was play
it had a terrible urgency to it.

Red St. Valentine

The fine flurry of red-Valentine's day, who
allowed Roman soldiers to marry and so angered
old Claudius Caesar that he had him martyred.
Heart so big, love of God so great, that I
sat in second grade hoping that Freddie
would send me his, would put a special
valentine in the crepe wrapped box with the
jagged slit; that I would get red lumpy valentines
from everyone, more than anyone, a population
of red hearts, but the biggest, the laciest,
the one most smeared and puckered
with paste would be from Freddie
and his fine awkward hand would inscribe it
with undying love

Once he gave me a shaped box, red
with gold trim and I kept it long
after the chocolates were poked,
identified and eaten, a fingered dimple
in the bottom, deep
as the dimple in Freddie's chin,
the little Kewpie swirl of his hair
on top of each chocolate.

SLIDE SHOW II

For when I remember the library on the corner of
Bedford and Pacific, next to the Presbyterian church
where my father had once been assistant minister
inside the stone-blocked walls before I was born,
and where he met my mother; all this next to the
Stamford library not five blocks from my house, the
elements of my escape lined Dewey-decimaled on
shelves and I went weekly, leaving the dog tied to
an outside railing, patient with occasional yips of
not-patient, and I bent selecting, my mother's
admonition ringing in my ears, *One good book before
you turn to Walter Farley and Howard Pease.* Then I
remember how I longed to wander in tall adult
stacks across the building where librarians did not
know my name and looked forbidding if I crossed
their threshold sanctorum.

Savings Account

During the war we saved twine,
each member of the family, her own ball
started from grocery parcels.

It was for the soldiers
or maybe being careful.
Balls of string sat on the sideboard
next to the rubber band balls
and the flickering balls of tin foil
and to one side, for army blankets,
the rising piles of olive squares
woven on picket-prongs.

It was our bureau of concern,
our attention to common things,
to packaging and waste,
of what had been,
and what could win a war.

1943

Over there, somewhere,
in lands we haven't studied,
is a war swallowing men.
We know the enemy,
dirty krauts, yellow japs,
fight them in the woods, the swamps
of my friends' back yards.

Men with square faces
and buck teeth who want to kill me.
In and out of the woods we attack
and retreat, careful
of skunk cabbages we call land mines.

Our hatred is unbridled.
We are right, we Yanks.
We have the best planes, red, white and blue
targets painted on wing tips.

With my small metal helmet, my red and blue
CD button, I go out after dark with my mother
to patrol streets for chinks of light
that might show all the way up through the sky,
to planes with black crosses
and red bulls' eyes.

Spattered among the windows are ribbons,
sons and husbands gone to war,
Gold Star Mothers, sons who will not come back.

Germans in our town, once neighbors,
are eyed with suspicion. Mr. Schneider
who repaired our clocks and watches
peering squint-eyed through his tiny telescope,
now with no customers, takes his delicate springs,
crystals and watch stems, and retreats
behind his curtained window.

Steel Rings

I

I watch the steel rings
of the magician –
  CLANG, CLANG, he goes
to show us they are solid,
joined inexorably
one to the other to the other
and the trick is to make them separate,
to hold them aloft in the expectant air.

II

Every school morning we drove,
my mother and I, to the next town
where she taught and I learned,
leaving my grandmother
to the freedom of a day without us
whom she had taken in
when my father died young.

En route we picked up Miss Moore
who taught second grade
and one year taught me,
and each day as she approached the car,
chattering like a chickadee,
I felt the circle of my mother
slip outside of mine and separate.

III

Last week my cousin, Deirdre
brought two friends to our cabin
on the lake with the blue Indian name.
They talked and one said,
The best teacher I ever had was Miss Moore.

Then she and my mother, sixty years apart,
reminisced,
and into the warm smell of Jeffrey pine
drifted the circle-breaking smell
of burnt toast and coffee,
which always pushed into our car with Miss Moore,
into the front seat,
where I had been sitting,
into the circle where I had been linked:
      from the back seat,
      from the summer cabin,
      from across the years,
I could hear the crunch of toast,
the sharp Boston twang
and feel the circles clink apart.

If I'd walked to school,

slid out the oak door
and begun the hike to the ridge
where the school bricks shone
like a sailor's warning,
where the houses I passed
might have contained children I knew,
their parents, their kitchens,
we might have become a millipede of scholars
working our irregular path up the hill,
timing the lift of our shoes
to avoid pavement cracks that might harm our mothers.

But I didn't walk to school, didn't know
if there were other girls waiting to be my friend,
houses of boys like Freddie, who might admire
the oiled pocket in my fielder's glove.

War Effort

During the war, my mother
rolled bandages, day after day,
stretchy pink things like cloth.
She would bring home the seconds,
while I knit blanket squares
of scratchy olive-drab wool, stacked them
like pancakes on the dining room table,
an inedible color, an unwearable roughness.

Enough to be a soldier
in a muddy trench, living with death
and the fear of not measuring up;
even if sleep might come,
the scratchiness of those squares
would surely drive it off.

This was not the comfort I wanted to send
to handsome dark-haired lovers
I imagined waiting for letters from me,
their square jaws lit by the flash of bombs.
I wrote the letters long and ardent,
but there was never anyone
to send them to.

My Grandmother's Kitchen

I never went in the kitchen
when Annie was our housekeeper
unless heading through the back passage
down the wide steps to the yard.

But Annie was gone. Mother was tired,
teaching all day, bandaging at night.
The kitchen stayed the same – creamy
white walls, big wooden table in the center
with grain drawers that opened down like yawning
mouths, rattling with a few potatoes, onions.

In one corner the tall hutch, where a turn
of the crank snowed out sifted flour. My
grandmother liked baking. Maybe she was glad
Annie had been swallowed by the war.

Grammy became dredged in flour, a virago
of pie crusts and cakes, dumplings and roast chicken
and together we went to the butcher,
*See that it's ground beef and not
horsemeat. I know you, Andy Henson.*

★

To Granelli's for vegetables and grains.
I would make a village of roads by dragging my
shoe through the sawdust. Mr. Granelli
had a trolley ladder attached to his shelves
and would spring aboard as the ladder raced
down the length. I thought it fine as any fair ride.
Then he would look grave and give me
a pickle from the barrel.

Sometimes we walked all the way down Pacific
where the side walks were sawdust, and crates
lay broken open, fish stacked and chickens
and the smell thick and rank and I would be
in a hurry to get home even if it meant
plucking pin feathers from cold pimpled skin.

When the war ended, Mother cried.
We went out onto Forest Street and danced
with neighbors and strangers. Sugar and butter
returned. But not Annie.
The kitchen had changed hands for good.

The Monster in the Cellar

Our cellar was distant country,
high windows overgrown by vines,
corners thick with cobwebs,
and no one liked the coal room
where soot stirred at the slightest breeze.

In the center, like a fortress
was the furnace, scabby gray,
its black mouth clanked shut, iron bar
across its grin.

Winter, when it roared for food,
my grandmother hefted the shovel
and fed it. I crept
half-down the stairs to see it open
its ferocious red mouth
and gulp black chunks like candy.

Deep in its throat the red wavered and sucked,
flicking its forked tongue, forcing
my grandmother to retreat. She held
the shovel like a lion tamer's whip
then nudged the mouth shut with a clang.

On any floor you could feel
the monster's heavy step. The house shuddered
when he woke, relaxed when he slept.
He seeped up stairs, under doors,
settled on sills and tables.

My grandmother cursed him
as best she dared
while she wiped a white cloth into gray
with the grime of his oily breath.

Religion in a Seed

Sunday School was the weekly millstone.
Dresses that made me feel sticky,
patent leathers with a narrow strap
and one round button
to be sure they stayed on.
On Sundays, the socks must be white,
no yellow or pink line around the cuff.

I knew I had to go for my father,
who had left his clarinet,
his clerical robes, and sermons
stacked in a box in the attic,

And for my mother. I must be good
and God would help me.
I must learn His stories, most of which
were either boring or not possible.

I was fervent for a while
about the mustard seed
rattling around in a little plastic globe
with a brass 'belt'.
Here, at last, was hope.
If I had as much faith
as this grain of mustard seed, all things
would be possible.
I had a chance.
I didn't need dead men
walking around three days later.
I just needed a faith tiny as a seed,
and I had that;

I had faith that Freddie loved me
and that Bobby Jordan would always
smell bad. I had faith that I would
be passed to fourth grade, and yes,
I was pretty sure the sun would come up.

The Mantras of the Mother

My mother single parent living with her mother feared the wolf that whistled at the door certain that he licked his chops for me and the more my legs readied to fly the more migraines Mother seemed to get *Don't let a boy touch you* Oh that was early on and *boys don't like girls who are too smart* and *for heaven's sake, don't be so athletic you'll get a mannish reputation* and *Heed me now, don't beat the boys at tennis or basketball don't befasterorstronger don't talkdirty, don't listentothosethatdo. Oh dear, John's mother said you told John a dirty joke* and *don't* she said *speak up too much in class* and *Oh no, Charlie's mother says Charlie won't play tennis with you anymore, because you always beat him* Well who said I to drive her mad, wants to play tennis with someone you always beat and *watchoutforDemocrats, don't talktomenonthesubway theymightbewhiteslavers,* and *don't walkoutsidealone,* and watch out the sky is falling and *becarefulofboysfromthatpartoftown, never mixplaidsandstripes, only black girls mix red and pink, only Catholic girls wear pierced earrings, and stop for goodness sake bitingyournails*

Girls and Horses

I remember Emily Evans
in third grade, the first
of the riding crop girls, galloping
through Red Rover and Dodgeball,
ponytail bobbing to the gait,
her flanks constantly lashed
by an applewood sapling.
And how she whinnied,
big yellow teeth and velvet muzzle
curled as she called to other horses
far off in the fields along Mansfield Avenue.

Boys stepped back
away from the speed and intensity
of Emily at full gallop,
unconsciously aware that something
was happening before their time.

The girls fluttered as if exposure
was here, and they might step in it.

In Junior High, rich girls
with velvet hard hats and their own horses,
strode impeccably on the grounds
of the Ox Ridge Hunt Club
in smart jodhpurs and well-shined
always-new boots, and their hair
smelled of money.

Emily and I went to Self's,
a place of blue uniforms
with red stripes lining the legs,
uniforms of cavalry and caissons.
We had to march for half an hour
around the ankled dust of the indoor ring.
Complete with privates to captains,
we were close-ordered and right-flanked,
and snapped-to; an effort to turn us
into men before we mounted the horses
and rode off into our sexuality.

Hopscotch

I had the perfect pebble,
almost a square
a rounded pillow of a square
and it was cream-colored
with a green line
that ran across in one direction
and a black line
that crossed it the other way
like an Xmas present.

I kept it in my pocket
rubbing it for luck before a math test
or before making the first toss
into the eight squares
drawn on the playground.

In those days
I could balance on one leg
like a heron in a swift moving stream.
I could bend
as in ballet and pause
above the pebble,
pick it up delicate as a mule
nibbles grass,
unwind, and hop on my way.

I was so good at hopscotch,
the other girls began to eye
my magical pebble as the source.
They made up rules such as –
winner gets to choose a pebble, or

no pebbles with stripes.

SLIDE SHOW III

For when I remember the first dancing class,
our first ball gowns (how I hated mine) blue with
white eyelet lace and off the shoulder; what
would hold it up, surely not those two pebbles
finally poking their way through my earth; the new
worries of necklines too low, strapless bras too high
in the back, horrible boning that stuck into tender
skin, and that was just the top; below, hidden under
the hated eyelets, and the pale – so feminine – blue,
was a Middle Ages torture of crinolines, made of
stiff plastic netting never properly finished so every
inch harbored a prickle to scratch the legs, snag
stockings, make rustling sounds, a giraffe caught in
the hunter's net. Then I remember how this
treacherous crinoline kept me from dancing too
close to the boys, for as you pressed near, it rose
behind revealing all, and if you weren't careful as a
monk when you sat down, it would rise up in front,
higher and with less dignity.

The Silk Scarf

I know little about you
a spattering of stories
courage and illness

some pictures of you
forever young
blond hair and a thin face

black and white or sepia
wearing your graduation gown
with the white fur collar

or tennis sweater and always
long pants because it was the style
because you lost a leg

to the cancer
that killed you before I
blew my first candle

I used to yearn that you
were only away
would come in a Spitfire

to land in our field
and swoop me up
your white silk scarf

billowing over your leather shoulders
and you'd take me to fly
above the valleys

Women Brushing Hair

In the front room, my grandmother
would brush her hair, long and blue-white.
She sat in the window
watching street life, her brush moving
rhythmically, sliding through the white strands
brushing   brushing,
hypnotic as cobra music.
Was she thinking of my grandfather? Had he
brushed it for her?

No one brushed my hair, long
loving strokes to my waist
making it sizzle, fly away charged
with its own engine.
Oh, my mother brushed
before she twisted it into braids
that popped my eyes, filled with
late for school, fidgets, and snarls
that caught the brush in a battle of pulling.
Finally she had it cut off and curled
with home permanents so snaggly
that brushing made no difference.

I have never brushed my mother's hair.
It would make her uncomfortable
to be so intimate.
I didn't have a sister but we might
have brushed for each other. She would have been
dark like my mother and if our father had lived
he might have liked our hair long.
Her brush full of trailing black hair, and mine
almost as white as my grandmother's
at the opposite end of years.

Small as I was, I admired my grandmother's hair,
the inward place she went when she brushed, the gleam
as it took on the shine of well-polished metal
like the silver-backed brushes moving gently
but intently through her hair,
embossed initials catching in the light.

Hidden Up

In the center of the yard,
like a gift from Jack and his six beans:
a chestnut worthy of the village smithy.

Its vast trunk crowns well above
the third story and the roof.
Each spring it unfurls its celadon mittens

that turn into green spaniel ears,
and white spikes of flowers
shoot up like fountains.

Once I learn to get up that tree
I creep and climb
behind the shadow of leaves.

From the kitchen window I hear
family voices murmur; from the porch
the creak of wicker, squeak of the green glider.

In my tree I am sailing the South Pacific,
fighting enemies in jungles and small villages,
or writing smudgy notes to Freddie.

As the sun takes its slow, western course
dappling through branches until it reaches
the break in the leaves that means supper.

Annie's Room

I wanted to sleep in the attic,
in the special room where Annie
once slept under the eaves.
Annie long-gone into war factories
south of the tracks.

My mother said no,
because of fire she said,
so I practiced crawling out
the small window
onto the slanted roof, calculated
the leap to the chestnut tree.

I wanted to be near my father.
He was stored in boxes
in the tower room: his books,
sermons, black robe, his clarinet
with silver bands, silver keys

and in a corner, the gilded bust
my mother made, surreal:
the mask of a missing man,
missing arms, shoulders,
missing heart.

Baseball

On TV, the ball is perfect, laced like yin and yang around the sphere, leather taut, the weight, the heft known to each pitcher's fingers, the rub of his palms, spread of his grip controlled for sliders, drop, fast ball the inside curve. For us, it was a field scraggly with spring-grown and the hidden mine fields of neighborhood dogs, the ball no longer white, might not even be round, probably sneaked from a brother's supply of rejects, the leather as near to mud as mud, and the stitches if not already torn, likely to splay on the third hit. Moreover, it would be lopsided from too many whacks of Jimmy Sydon's bat and so when pitched to us took a seductive wobble no pitcher intended and sometimes, if older brothers were stingy or home – we resorted to tennis balls, smaller, springier, which if we connected drove far beyond the left fielder with zest but without that satisfying thunk of a true hit; easy pickings for Sparkplug a rangy setter who somewhere had a secret hoard we never found. No matter the ball, its condition, its tendency to drift, baseball was our life, filled our afternoons and into the dusk of mosquitoes and ignored dinner calls. We knew the players on our favorite teams, could time our movements to the up-flung foot of Preacher Roe, the long languid stretch off first base of Gil Hodges. We shielded our eyes with our ratty old gloves, Duke Snider roaming center field.

Greviously Greens

We all learned the shades of white that got us out of trouble, and the blues were Saturday nights without a date – again, and Holly Golightly's mean reds were scary, close to an edge that seemed to pull us over into darkness. I was, however, fond of the grievously greens, those moments of envy over Judy's sweater set, that my fingers itched to snag a little string and unravel it from behind. The greens lived in junior high, lingered in the halls, and wafted from our locker grates. They swirled around the Lee jeans that Barb and Jane had, well, all the girls in all the world, except me. Lee's had a blank patch of leather near the belt where you could tattoo your name (or someone's), an upgrade from writing a boy's name on your palm, which didn't last, and besides my jeans came from Greenberg's Super Shopper and even the stitching was the wrong color. Since my father was long dead, and no brothers, I had no man's shirt to wear over my stitch-betrayed jeans, long tails out, sleeves rolled half way up my arms in perfect folds, and though I was pitcher on our baseball team, my mitt was some kind of thin, fake leather, held together by prayers, while Libby who was only third base, had a Carl Furillo signature glove, in which she put a hard ball of her brother Ted's and rubber bands to hold it closed. I did that too, but it didn't matter, my glove was more like a dinner plate, and so I carried the grievously greens before me like a dowsing stick, searching and searching for disappointments.

Tomboy

In my family
I was a tomboy
needing a bridle of lace.

No one
would have given me
a football
no matter how many times
I put it on my birthday list.

But I had an old,
windfall football,
not full size
or good weight,

and I could loft
a perfect spiral
to the farthest end
of the driveway
right to Libby
who gathered it in.

Sudden Caress of Cinnamon

When I am surprised by cinnamon, I remember
        Christmas in a white Connecticut, where
        snow clings to the right angles of branches
        and windows.
I remember the grog burbling like birds in the silver
        server and the poker resting in the embers.
I can conjure the plunge of the poker, the roil of brew,
        the hot flights of cinnamon, her sisters,
        clove and nutmeg, hugging the air.
And I remember my dark mother, young and laughing –
        bringing in platters and the amber carafe of brandy,
        the spice of her, the spiced air with a tinge of apple,
And I remember the missing space of my father,
        the solid lack of him,
        the way the cinnamon parts
        and leaves him defined by absence.

spitting

black slippery seeds   at cousins

at my mother   in a spume   of bravado   green   hard

fat blimp of a fruit   wavery black lines   like the bottom of the pool

full of water   red   red dotted Swiss   with black pips   and a border of white

fading to celadon   big bites   drool on the chin   down the neck   under the sleeveless

blouse   spitting   all that wind force   seeds   against your face   your dark shoulders

your hand hard   hard on my arm   watermelon   iced   in a washtub   floating

bobbing   chilled   sun-licked top   watermelon   porcupined with straws   gin

through the plug in the top   gin-full   gin full of air   red-water juice

a transfer of gin   from green dirigible   to our veins   laughter

gurgles   lights out   quiet   muffled giggles

watermelon summer

The Day My Uncle Dies

one of the last men in our family, all the women wait on the porch, my grandmother, apron dredged with flour, my aunts, their mouths set like city streets. A fierce line of women watch my mother park the Chevy, watch us get out, the jingle of keys, my face smudged from a long day in New York, voice rising to tell them about the Statue of Liberty, how we all *climbed to the torch on laddery stairs except Glenna who wouldn't, got left behind, cried so we could hear her all the way up* until my mother's hand falls firm on my shoulder. Aunt Marian takes my arm, turns me over to Annie who waits behind the screen door. I strain to see Mother surrounded, a sparrow harried by her kin of hawk-women. Annie, answering no questions, takes me to the kitchen where dinner will not be ready, makes cinnamon toast and pours frothy milk from a glass bottle.

★

The house is on tiptoes, the third tread creaks, doors close softly and I am always on the other side. I don't remember my mother coming to tell me Uncle Francis is dead, but Aunt Marian says gruffly, because this is her nature, *You can cry if you want to.* What's wrong with me? I am supposed to feel very sad, but he has left no space yet. At school I tell my friend Libby; we look knowing and shake our heads in a losing kind of way but nothing feels heavy the way it hangs on my mother, her eyes, rims red and soggy, or my grandmother, several lace handkerchiefs tucked here and there in her clothing, peeking out, sodden little birds of linen, or my aunt who goes from tears to tight rips of anger at *that woman, she drove him too hard.* I don't know what it means. Aunt Hazel doesn't like to drive and anyway she's home. Uncle Francis died in Hartford, a heart attack on the steps of the Capital. I can picture him there, sprawled in his brown suit, his big body taking up three or four steps, the dome shining above him.

The Funeral

I didn't know I'd be expected to look
at a dead body – that my tall uncle
with his gravel voice and laugh
will lie in a box-like bed lined with sheets
and I will be led to the front of the church
with my cousins to *pay my last respects.*

I don't have any respects,
don't know what they are
but I've read enough Tom Sawyer to know
I don't want to see any dead body.
What if it's naked?
I'm not supposed to see naked people,
not at the movies,
not the man in the woods
that made my mother run,
yanking me behind her.

In the church aisle, I drag my feet
as the box gets closer, closer, so that parts
of my uncle begin to rise – first his nose,
then the fingers of his hands, finally
the broad range of his forehead
and ears. By now I am close enough
to see that what is in the box
is no one I know
and then we're past, it's over,
and the only thing I've recognized
is the brown suit.

Magical Ten

First, I suppose, there are the horses,
hot, sweaty, their teeth green
from the grass I can't keep them from eating,
and the blue jeans I can wear to ride
but not to school or parties, and new Keds
to launch the summer, soft and bendy,
good for running, good for being in boats,

and the briny smell of the tide
and coast life, things clinging to rocks,
things in crevices waving claws or feelers
and I love the horseshoe crabs, that they
lumber and are prehistoric, and if you
turn one on its back, it does this
amazing thing with its tail,
jabs it in the sand like a pole vaulter
and flips its big old self over to safety.
And I like the first unfurling leaves of maple
so green they hurt my eyes, and later
the seed pods we'll open and stick
on our noses like hood ornaments,

and I love the notes we write to each other
in class and going back to school where I see
Freddie every day, and a new pencil case,
newly sharpened pencils with my name
in gold letters, that my aunt
gave me last Christmas, and of course my
mother only let me have two at a time,
so I have some new this September,

and the library where I go every week,
a better world there than my boring existence.
People in books always have
brothers and sisters – and persistence.

And the thunderstorms, great cracks
of lightning forking down over the house
across the street where skinny, mean Mrs. Gillespie
lives and I hope it will set her on fire
but instead it hits the church steeple
which bursts into flames – exciting –
before they put up the lightning rod,

shutting the barn door after the horses have flown,
sniffs my mother.

And buttered bread with brown sugar, and
tomatoes off the vine with Wonderbread
and Hellman's mayonnaise, and the x-ray machine
at Spelke's where I become acquainted
with the bones of my feet, and Spin the Bottle,
though the bottle is not a trusted friend, and
the hayrides, and Freddie's dry lips, and
his hot hand in mine.

SLIDE SHOW IV

For when I remember the salt-puckered skin
of summers spent on the Sound with halyards and
centerboards, and cleats that ripped shorts, and
telltales whipping useless around the stays, how
besotted we were with Bill and Jocko, older men of
eighteen who taught sailing and tried to keep their
juices contained in this enmeshment of a tribe of
just pubescent girls. Then I remember I was gangly
and awkward, poorer than most so my blue jeans
were not the right brand, and my sneakers were
sensible low-cost from Greenberg's, and I was not
among the first to need a bra.

Twelve

Such a feeling
like grass growing, summer full of sails,
and this morning, piles of books in every classroom.
By the end of today our lockers
will smell like fresh ink and Miss Carter
will say *Open to the center, now press gently*
and we'll work our way left, then right,
breaking in new books, and how they'll look
in June covered with notes and doodles,
Freddie's and other boy' names written on the edges.

War is barely over
and we have sugar again.
No more Civil Defense tin hat,
no more black-outs, no more saving
string, and tin foil,
no more weaving olive blanket squares
on those little metal prongs.
Although Mrs. Greenly still has her star flag
in the window for dead Peter,
we have white bandages again
and chewing gum
and gasoline without ration tickets.
And sugar.

Where Are My Men?

Where are my men
that should be in photos,
smiling disingenuously,
squinting in strong light?
They should be patting my head,
shadow-jawed, hair tousled,
even a little distant
and awkward.
Where are my men?
There should be grandfathers,
a father,
brothers,
with scratchy chins
and gruff voices,
disapproving voices
followed by easy smiles.

Where is the grandfather
with penny candy in his coat
and a big turnip watch
tucked snug in the pocket
just under his belt
where I could touch bottom
with one finger?
A father
to hand out chores
or give me a quick fond look
before scaring my date?
Never there.
They were never there –
any of them.
And I knew it,
daily from the least bone,
to the beat in my chest,
that they should be,
that they needed to be.

Freddie Speaks Up

He asks me out; could we got to a move? He will pay, he says. In the pocket of his brown corduroys, he has the quarters – shiny as his face, as his teeth, signaling his happiness, above the deep cleft in his chin; so deep he doesn't seem baked yet, his mother having pushed his chin to see if he was done, and left this captivating dimple that never goes away. I want to go, and I've loved him since kindergarten when he shared his straws because I could get in trouble with Miss Klein for unraveled milk straws.

Living far from each other, far from the theater, we have a problem, but my mother, bless her, not much given to dates in fifth grade and not much given to Freddie either, who lives in the poor section of town and has bad teeth, and whose mother takes in sewing because his father has died on a field in France and because I plead so, my eyes puffy and red with the love of Freddie, Mother agrees to drive. When we get to Freddie's I climb in the back seat where he will hold my hot hand with his hot hand and we will stare straight ahead.

But Freddie has brought a gift, hefting it down the four front steps of his house, both arms around it, hugging it really, his thin boy arms hugging a container of glass, shiny in the dusklight that falls around us softly, round the black Chevy sedan and me in the back seat waiting for Freddie and my mother in the front seat, looking bemused, I suppose, at this small elfin boy I love and the movie now forgotten, unlike the glass jar, enormous, the kind we used to get at warehouse sales, full of mayonnaise or pickles, thick glass to get it through many hands on its way to Freddie. His smile wide and the jar's mouth wide, the movement in the jar slowly available, the flicker of live things like gray spoons, the small coffee spoons my grandmother gets out after dinner to go with the tiny porcelain cups. The jar now revealing more movement than water, Freddie's mouth grows wider and my mother begins to shift uneasily. "Look," he says through the open door, "for you," he says, "I spent all afternoon at Tilley's Pond," he says, and carefully sets the full jar between us and climbs in, and even in the wake of his slim weight, a million pollywogs slosh together.

Mrs. Hendee

Your worst fears:
steely eyes, mouth made to hold pins,
a graying bun which pulled
her hair back tight as steel
and she had one of those knuckles,
like a thimble of rock
that she'd crack against your head
for talking, or even grinning;
one minute at the board chalking away,
the next beside you, wicked finger rapping.
No one wanted to be in her class,
inevitable, looming, sixth grade.

But I knew things about Mrs. Hendee:
why she was absent three days in April
and it was this. Her husband
painted the toilet seat, and forgot to mention it
and women being constructed as they are,
she must in time sit – and sit she did.

It was delicious. It was wildfire.
Mother swore me to secrecy
but there are some promises that can't be kept,
not in sixth grade, not with Mrs. Hendee
slicked on a wet, toilet seat,
white, I believe.

For days we discussed how she got off.
if she got off, who got her off and did he live
to tell the tale. Oh yes. I tell you,
it made school worthwhile for a month –
even fractions.

Other Peoples' Pictures

Two little girls in fluffy white dresses, sleeves puffed into wings.
Sisters.
A word I cherish.

An uncomfortable baby
held askew by her big brother
wishing the picture-taking over.

Another child sits on her grandfather's knee;
family groups of four or more.
I have none of these.

No father, grandfather,
no brother to tease.
No sister-ally.

No rough beards, no watch pockets
to hide a secret coin, no deep chuckle
that might have taken my side.

No one to teach me the finer points
of trees, no one to confide in,
argue with, tattle on.

Another picture:
small girl sits hunched on the back steps,
toes pointing together, face sad.

Although her hair is dark,
the steps different, another house,
I know that child

and the long afternoon shadows that crawl
across the grass and up the stairs,
the falling sun in her eyes.

Flying Up

Maroon and gold forever,
onward, onward to victory...

When we got to junior high
we left behind the smell of hot crayons
and fingerpaint; we chewed bubble gum
instead of school paste; we didn't
dig our fingers into fresh tar anymore
because we had allowances now,
could buy small pink rectangles of DoubleBubble
from Frate's Corner store.

Junior high smelled
of sweat, chemicals and fear;
doors were larger, halls cavernous.
We exchanged the smell of Bobby Harmer
pooping his pants, for Mike Graebler's
man-smell of staying back two times.

The buddy-boys of third grade
suddenly rumbled in our blood.
We began to learn
about moist hands and soft lips.
There were reasons now to stay after school.
New reasons for telephones
weekends, and diaries.

There was loud boy-talk
and secret girl-whisper;
we could go to the evening movies
without our parents.
We discovered close dancing
and darkened rooms.
We were on our way
and we knew it –
riding an off-shore current.

Capture the Flag

My mother and Mrs. Kelley,
workhorses of our Saturdays
before football weaned us to mud-smeared uniforms,

would fill the cars with wriggling boys
and girls, red-faced with anticipation
of bodily contact.

We would drive
over the New York border to Pound Ridge,
where trees had been planted in rows

and the slanted sun of spring or fall
cast arrows across the field of battle.
The game was Capture the Flag –

the object of the game:
to snatch the other team's flag
without being taken prisoner.

The object of the day:
to be chased by boys
and fall in a heap, with their humid

angular bodies on top of us –
those brief moments of contact flaming our cheeks
and imaginations.

Was it better to be on the same team
with Danny, plotting strategy,
because I was good at games,

or on the other side, plotting strategy
that would tease Danny to chase me
even if he'd rather chase Judy.

Leaves tickled down our necks, stuck to our
shirts and jeans, our faces flushed with fire,
our muscles taut, our lungs

bursting for gulps of air, our hearts beating
like crazed tom-toms, and Mother and Mrs. Kelley
nodding their heads and remembering.

Thirteen

So here we are, newly teened,
      with hot wax holding our wings in place,
and it's summer, the sails flap like large sheets
      where they hang in the sail loft
smelling salty from the race
      and walking through them is magical
like Don Quixote in a field of windmill vanes.
      Here are the clews ready for the shackles
here are the battens ready to brace the sails
      to hold a pocket of wind,
here are the halyards ready to be tightened and

here we are young, eager, girls
      all in love with the sailing teachers
their 18-year faces with a glint of bristle
      at the end of the day, their skins
tanned and wind-roughed and their
      sexuality absolute in every bone and muscle.
And I remember how we flared open in sunlight,
      took our small boats out on the Sound
and let lifts and headers knock us this way and that.
      You can chase a boy in a boat and never seem to.

Here are the horrible truths about 13 –
     The spot of blood that eats like acid
through your underpants to show up
     on the outside of your shorts
like the mark of Hester Pryn.
     Here is your washboard chest that shows
no sign of swelling, not like Sandy
     who's been with her mother to Greenberg's
and gotten a Double AA, and stuck her new
     barely-there shape forward like a frigate bird
until we got so riled, we ran her Double AA
     up the flag pole while she was swimming.

And here is Jimmy sitting on the dockhouse
     his legs open like pick-up sticks
and his balls, his nuts, his rubbery agates
     tumbling outside his shorts – lichee nuts
like those Mr. Chee gave us with our laundry
     and I couldn't take my eyes off Jim's
being from a family of women – this mystery
     a kind of gift – until Freddie whispered
and Jimmy clapped shut the barn door
     but it was enough.

So I remember being under the float
     and Skipper Dawes trying to kiss me
and it was nice to be wanted, but
     did it have to be Skipper, who looked
like a flounder and was always moist.
     And we weren't supposed to go under the float.
It was scary, but it made our mothers crazy

and I didn't like getting dunked
>how a boy would push you under
and then stand on your shoulders
>to jackknife you down even deeper
and the pilings shot past, a rush of barnacles
>and green crabs, as you sank into endless pewter
with just enough breath left
>to return to the surface
where someone always waited
>to rub jellyfish in your hair.

SLIDE SHOW V

For when I remember the hot back seats of junior high submarine races of high school, steamed windows and high anxieties; when I remember swaying in dark dens and basement playrooms to *Bewitched, Bothered, and Bewildered* and *Shrimp Boats Is A' Comin'*, reveling in sweaty cheek to cheek but peering into dimness to see how far other couples were going. Then I remember how the spring of tenth grade was *ruined* when my grandmother confused Pete with Freddie, gave away the game of two boys from different towns, and both of them huffed off into long grass, fading from my life – at least for then – how I shrieked with impotent fury when I found her reading my diary (this is how she knew) – and worst of all, she was laughing.

Some Knowledge of Water Shared

I was sorry for people who had to rely on pools,
who thought the wavy black lines were bottom,
who thought the diving board was distance, who
would have cringed to share water with creatures.

In pools, the only unknown was how it felt
to fill with water and sink. Where I swam
was compelled by the moon itself. Tides
turned twice a day a little later.

Where I swam was more than stroke and flutter kicks,
more than breathe on the right, it was
stinging eyes, and once your eyes adjusted it was
objects behind a scrim.

Jellyfish floated beneath the surface,
latitudes of pale stripes along their bodies.
You could almost see through them, you could
catch them in your hands, bring them out of water
where they filled with gravity
and slid through your fingers back home.

No place safe for feet. Every cranny and surface
covered with tidal accommodation. Barnacles
crusting the rocks withdrew
their delicate feelers at your shadow and closed
their sharp cutting surfaces.

Slime and flowing seaweed prevented footholds,
crabs waved their front claws from pilings: things
that can't live in chlorine, things that need slots
and overhangs, need seagrass and rough surface.

When we jumped off the pilings into the deep end
we trusted that the solid blue below would part
and let us through, would close over as if
we belonged, as if we needed to be at the bottom
and when our lungs and legs shoved us back toward sky
the water parted again to let us loose.

Saturday Matinees on the Post Road

Saturdays were the mating rustle and the best place for that was matinees at the Playhouse on the Post Road. We knew the songs by heart: *Tea for Two, Once in Love with Amy Smoke Gets in Your Eyes.* We knew the dancers: Kelly, O'Conner, Astaire. We saw the soft gauzy heroines, Garland, Day, Grayson and singers Keel, Sinatra, Crosby, and we knew who sat with whom in orchestra and loge. From Saturday to Saturday the line-ups changed in our rows of seats. Moist hands were held, arms crept tentatively across the backs of seats onto shifting or receptive shoulders. Our faces were straight ahead, eyes on the screen where the true romance we aspired to took place weekly, aching misunderstandings we knew led to dreamy looks and chaste kisses. Serious 'steadies' meant segregation from the group. Necking with Freddie went on in the balcony, paying little attention to the movie. Later we'd get knowing looks and twinges of envy. Junior high magic before we graduated to high school, when football games took over Saturday afternoons and movies moved more seriously to Saturday nights.

Sweet Shoppe

Raucous
from sitting more or less still
we burst from the dark theater
into afternoons existing in real time.

Our romance indicators were high,
some surreptitiously rubbed their faces
to remove smudged lipstick,
couples sprang apart by gender
and we laid siege on the Sweet Shoppe.

With mixed feelings they watched us come.
Even our meager allowances
made business good, but the anticipated
devastation... Straw papers flew
across the room. How else to know
he likes me if he doesn't toss a French fry
into my hair. Sodas spilled
and sloshed across tables.

While waiting for our orders we played 'salts' –
salt-shaker shuffleboard.
Like little glass lighthouses,
we slid them across the table
to see how close to the edge we could get.

One point if you could run the top joint
of your thumb along the table edge
and touch the salt cellar. Two points
if it hung over the edge.

Polio

Polio is eating children,
licklipping round our friends, while parents
rip our immortality with hot breath.
  Avoid crowds.   Don't get over tired.
  No swimming.   Do your legs ache?

Polio stalks the sand, likes to catch the unwary
trotting home from school. In the uneven battle
to protect, our parents have helpless eyes.

We sit in homeroom, as the ripples spread.
Look anxiously at each other, *Did you hear?*
Three from one family. Yesterday.
The twins have Paralytic. And Roy,
locked in with Bulbar, an all
or nothing fight. Only Devin escapes,
guilt-wrapped in his luck.

The bell clangs us to science. Halls buzz
with polio's icy reach. Bulbar freezes Roy
in its twenty-four hour grip. We know it's death
or recovery. Crippled Janie and Pete take a back seat
to the clenched fists in intensive care.

In Math, Mr. Benson announces, *No change.*
Girls crumple, boys go solemn, twitch.
The Deathwatch Beetle stirs.

Latin comes welcome. Energy of translation diverts us
from weightlessness. Miss Schaub drives hard,
keeps us outside ourselves with halting *agricola* and *te amo.*

We eat only low murmurings for lunch. And by History,
shiver in tightness. *Don't talk to us, don't touch us.*
We need our strength to urge toward Roy.

"ATTENTION, PLEASE," the loudspeaker squalls.
We startle from deep within, where we lie
curled around our certainties. "ATTENTION, PLEASE,"
from the webbed box high on the wall, above the clock,
I am happy to tell you that Roy Carter is out of danger.

Bricked in emotions explode the school in shouts, cheers.
Girls unstoppered, flow. Boys slap backs, punch the air.
Moments later, Mr. Kohler brings us down,
Can we return now to the Bill of Rights?

But Roy Carter has brought us face to fear with death.
Can we forgive him for that?

Skating

The ice is lumpy.
There are twigs embedded.
My blades are dull,
my ankles weak.
The air is crisp
like apples without taste.
My ears stick out
into the cold.
I lace my skates,
pull tight at the ankles.
My knees get wet.
They will get wetter.
I will be awkward,
a crane misjudging land.
The pond is dark slate
under a mica shield.
There are bumps and crackles.
My ankles touch the ice.
I look for Fred.
He has racing skates,
black leather, thick blades.

His ankles are vertical.
His nose is red.
He has a dimple I love.
I push off from shore
and fall flat.
I get better.
I crack the whip.
My breath billows.
My lungs heave.
I have a red scarf.
My breath catches in the wool
and freezes there.
My chin gets chapped
and my lips.
They'll be prickly.
Fred won't want to kiss them.
The pond is small.
We fill it with voices.
Our mothers made cocoa.
It rolls down our insides,
a fire against the chill.
Winter black and white.

Viewpoint

Summer was our bravest season. We wore
as little as possible given what
we began to possess. We were jealous
of Sandy, first to have a bra,
first to wear a bikini and not
look ridiculous

and Mr. Coons opened the summer
with a bikini of his own, slate blue
with cats cradles up both sides
where flesh surged out.

"Dis gusting,"

like a Greek chorus the mothers
clacked their alarm,
shuddered at the slick material –
the lattice work – but we knew

they were most afraid
of the bulges,
the explicit bullseye at the front.

No one was interested in jiggly
Mr. Coons. We liked to check on boys
whose swim trunks flared
as they sat back casually, legs
thrown about like jackstraws

and in the dark caves
of their groins
could be seen the soft
wrinkled globes of their – oh god – balls
as they rustled to one side, exposed
and raw, so entirely external.

Summer Photograph

There's a boat, such a small one
like a coracle, what we called a dinghy,
shaped as a bean seed, and there are
two girls, blonded into sunlight, their hair
disappearing in the air, and their faces
are tan, except for the wedge of zinc oxide
on each nose, noses that will pink
and peel anyway all summer.

We wear navy shorts with white side stripes,
hers are wider than mine and have extra buttons,
and we wear striped t-shirts, horizontal is fine –
it's after gaps in our teeth, but before breasts.
We smile like crazy, squinting; the more we squint
the wider we smile, it's connected, I tell you.

She has many teeth that don't fit in her mouth,
never mind, we are friends, our heads tilt together,
our shoulders are touching, the boat is rigged,
one mast, one sail. The centerboard is down,
rudder tilted in, tiller slipped under the traveler,
telltales are snapping, and waves kick at the boat
to get it started. We'll push off, skid over saltwater
chop chopping at the bow.

We'll leave mothers behind on the pier, on the dock,
straining their eyes at our distancing speck.
We'll heel over, sit on the windward rail, our seats
soaking up wave-splash. We'll be smiling
up at the sail, as we are smiling now
at the open lens of my mother's camera,
catching this moment, before…

SLIDE SHOW VI

For when I remember how I learned to drive
my mother ashen in the passenger seat, giving
uncontrolled gasps as I jerked the accelerator into a
cha cha cha, making my heart race even faster than
hers; how we struggled around and around the high
school parking lot, the boredom of small tight circles
and the constant stutter of starting in first, trying to
shift to second with the car doing a buck and wing to
my mother's moans. Then I remember how she got
so mad she made me get out *until I could behave,* and
magenta with rage, I watched her drive off. Knowing
she would go only around the corner; I took off on
another road, walked home from late afternoon into
dusk; two towns away, a long cold time but I scared
her and I didn't get my license that year.

The Tipsy Dance of Black Can and Red Nun

Sail and sail, with unshut eye. – Matthew Arnold

Red Right Returning, we'd say

in junior high summers,

      and skim off
            like windblown scut

flying over white caps of the Sound.

    Starboard Tack
      Close Hauled
        Leeward Boat

      Give Way, Give Way

We knew these things,
knew the rules
where we were heading
what to do on the way

at least for now.

     We trimmed our sails
        or payed them out, but we knew

      our fastest tack was a reach

cutting across the wind
         optimum of wind and sail surface

     and we liked to go fast.

Headers were momentary,
lifts too, they were for
careful close-hauled boats
following the courses
set out by committees.

We wanted dead ahead,

   racing

     flying,

       all out speed

 so fast you had to hang out to windward

          into the void.

For that long childhood time, my course
was lined with black cans and red nuns,
standing in narrow water courses
anchored to a dark sea bed.

And I never went to the Protest Committee
where 4-inch red and blue hulls
had a deck pole to show boom positions,
We slid them around the table like water skaters
to show the wrongs and rights of navigation
and rules.

  Did you touch?
  Did the boats touch?
    The crucial questions,
    the crux of racing.

I didn't go
because I knew the fault;
we did not touch enough
and I was, after all,
at the tiller of my own boat,
I sailed the course,
tacked when I should,
and I chose to reef my sails.

Now, as then
      I know the risks of rocks beneath

                  a surface

of what's revealed at lowering tide,
      of jelly fish that sting

          and when to push off from Turbin's Island

    or be stranded

        as surely as starfish,

and if I step,

      unwary,

on the spiny horseshoe crab

    his tail spiked at 45 degrees,

well, that's my look-out

        for sailing uncharted.

Shiners

Reluctant to let loose of summer,
we bring out our bamboo poles –
line and reel, sinker, red bobber

and hook. Every day after school,
we jump on our bikes and head for the Sound,
stopping at the Rod and Reel for chum.

Because nights fall faster now, and the
gray of homework hangs in the air,
we pedal hard right out the pier,

down the ramp to the dock, dig out
chum, sprinkle it in the water
and as it drifts oily, there is,

like a clap of hands, a frenzy
of minnows chewing and gulping.
We scoop them

in a net, into a bucket. I never
got used to putting minnows on my hook
and it wasn't the shiners,

bodies silvery with water running off.
They were good to eat but no one
really wanted to clean them.

It was the quiet smell of salt
and what tides do to a shore.
It was a clicking rustle of water

over barnacles and clusters of
purple mussels on the pilings. It was
the chuggle of waves

slapping under docks and floats,
an applause of sailboats not yet hauled,
spanking down their bows.

Gulls wheeled, the air crisp as Winesaps,
and the black bell-buoy tilted
up the waves and down into the troughs

clanging once each way. Our sweaters were red,
our hair blond, our blue jeans cuffed a
perfect two inches – Libby and I

turning summer into fall.

The Sap of Spring

He lit the buds, just forming on the branch-tips,
lit them like candles. The sap of spring
sizzled at the kiss of the match, sputtering,
a tree of buds that would not be candles, as if
his birthday wasn't enough, as if the sky –
nice rich blue – was a blowing wind
that snuffed candles for a living – nice tree,

its bark a ruffled pelt, skin outside skin,
like the summer tan that sloughs off in long
mica-ed sheets. We'd sit at the end
of the dock and peel the boys –
curling patches of them – want to keep them
in scrapbooks, but they had no substance,
were only the stuff of boys who smelled of salt
and hidden cigarettes.

We left their backs tattered like the pinto ponies
we rode on Wednesdays, aiming them
toward the low white fences, hoping
when they jumped they would use
their own good sense and not rely on
messages from our legs – nice ponies

with their mud-caked hoofs
we paten-leather-shined for gymkhanas,
reins loose on their necks, our nice
taut rumps tucked into English saddles,
rounding on the canter – nice leather smell,
rising like tree-sap under us – leather
and some primal woman-smell beginning,

nice smell, the boys thought
sneaking a sniff of saddles in the tack room
the way they used to smell our bicycle seats,
some aphrodisiac they would grow into,
boys with hot eyes that wanted things,
that talked about the things they wanted,
with a can of Bud and a Camel,
things they wanted but didn't yet know how to get –
the promise of nice things,

and the ponies, turned out to graze, nibbled
with their fat square teeth,
their nice muzzles soft against the hand
offering carrot, sugar cube,
their brown eyes half-lidded,
right legs cocked, – shapely legs –
better than Nancy Lexon's, whose legs
could do things to boys – nice boys –
but vulnerable as wheat before the reaper.

The little ponies with their yellow / green teeth,
and their whisk-tails chasing off flies,
brushed our faces, necks, shoulders,
teeth nuzzling, tails whispering –
nice tails – nice ponies.

with a bow to Gerald Stern

Freddie and the Leather Boys

They were the Post Road boys.
They lived in town, in houses that touched,
houses needing paint, and money for the rent.
We never talked of their parents,
what their fathers did.
We didn't know their families,
what they did on Sundays.

They were the boys who crossed themselves
before games, fingered the plated medals
around their necks. They were the boys
who cursed with horned fingers, or a fist
jammed in the crotch of an elbow.

They wore their hair in ducks' asses and smoked.
Their fingers were yellow at the tips
and their breath – their yellow breath.
They had cars, not the sturdy Plymouths
of our fathers, but well-tuned jalopies
they assembled at Elder's garage.
Turquoise or lime, with cracked seats
and a neckers' knob so you could ride close,
his left hand on the knob and his right hand
across your shoulder, sneaking forays
down toward your breast.

They were the boys our mothers
feared, older boys,
their bristles glistened in the afternoon light.
Our mothers rolled their eyes, kept those boys
off the party lists.

But they were there,
at all the parties – outside – in the katydid nights –
the rasp of a match – the flicker of cigarettes glowing –
the soft creak of leather jackets – their voices low
and the occasional bark of a laugh, quick, then gone.

Reading Dirty

Warped, wrinkled book passed hand to hand,
girls allowed only if we begged,
took it to a corner so no one would see us blush.
The Amboy Dukes – we read it beginning to end
for the one grubby page where the book fell open,
the boy putting his hand down her blouse,
fingering her bra before
cupping his way beneath it.

Later in Paris, we found our way
to Shakespeare and Company,
to a coverless paperback with uncut pages:
Lady Chatterley's Lover.
Could we get it through customs,
would the Catholic Church and the Protestant Fathers
line the docks when the ships pulled in –
the rollicking, leaky old student ships
refitted from war – each passenger
with the book, each reading, reading,
through Lawrence's long preamble,
to the pages – those few hot pages –
where she strews the flowers, arranges them…

All the deep, hot-cheeked longings,
tantalized in books, inflamed by their
very forbiddenness. Passion turning over
and over in new forms:
Forever Amber, Molly Bloom, Anaïs Nin,
as we careened through the school years
looking for ourselves.

Parallel Lives

Lined in rows like young gods, high school boys in uniform, basketball cupped between the captain's feet, Bill, and on the end, Freddie, my beloved, so cute, so sweet, so third-string. Large glossy team picture, matted, and for that season at least they lived in Valhalla, wore their letter sweaters, gave them to favored girls with curls and pink blouses. They left sixth period early to suit up while the rest of us groaned through Geography. For them we filled the gym on Friday nights, shouted, swooned, urged them on. It was our LSD, it was our Ecstasy.

On the lower field behind the school or in the gym on torpid afternoons, I played soccer, baseball, basketball. I kicked goals, scored free throws, so did Libby and Bets and Tina, so did Grace and Jean and Carol and Jane. We never got out of class, no framed pictures to be autographed and the audience was mostly teammates. A few mothers came, but not mine – athletics were no way to get a husband, did not impress colleges, might even keep me from the prom. But we had bodies in spite of our parents; though often admonished, we played to win.

I couldn't understand the way things worked. To be skilled and yet pretend otherwise, to be bright, but act uncertain. *Boys don't like to be bested,* she said, *Boys don't like girls to be athletic, They won't like you if you're too smart,* she said and I would feel the heel of her disapproval pressing on every part of me that moved outside the lines.

Longest Leap Outside Calaveras

Poor frog, split gut to nose, intestines uncontained, a population
of eggs swarms like amoebae across the lab tray. Donnie turns
greener than the late frog, slides delicately beneath the table.

We work that frog for a full week, less grid, less recognizable. I talk
through each step. Donnie keeps his eyes squeezed shut, takes
shallow breaths against the formaldehyde making him woozier
than those lost eggs.

One morning, we learn to pinch nerve bundles running along the
spine, and both legs flex at the knee like a ballerina. Donnie, who
has finally parted one eye in a sloe-eyed slit, jumps as if he's been
gaffed, lab tray takes flight and My Lady Frog makes her last
prodigious leap

to a place of authority – Dr. McAusland's desk. Detention for a week
– both of us.

Back Roads, One Hand on the Wheel

Where I grew up, back roads
were curvy with no shoulders, poorly graded
so the thank-you-ma'ams took your breath away
and threatened the undercarriage.

Boys had turquoise cars, or dulled maroon
with fins and twin beams, took the roads
like pebbles on a washboard. Our teeth
rattled and the steering wheel jumped
in the hands of backyard boys who fixed
their own cars, whose hands were grimed
with oil, hair doused with Brylcreem
until it bristled like quills.

Bobby's car was a dull pink coupe
already old and unsteady but the tires
had tread and the chrome
was polished like grandmother's silver.

The necker's knob
on the steering wheel at ten o'clock
let Bobby navigate the bumpiest road
with his left hand while his right
wrapped his girl like a boa constrictor.

Never have I ridden with anyone since
who could control cars
like Bobby and his friends.

While the *right* boys talked of baseball
and college, Bobby, Freddie, TomTom and Big Al
talked of grease, butterfly clutches, valves,
pistons and TurtleWax.

Roads of southern Connecticut were a menace
to be charged. Frost heaves buckled the Macadam
into ruptures and sink holes. Cracks ran hither
and yon like crackled glaze.

Two cars could pass – barely
and trees interspersed with stone walls
banked the roads into funnels of speed.

In winter, roads were slick, treacherous
from November to March, the only thing
that slowed pink cars and turquoise.

The High School English Teacher

Didn't want to babysit his children –
did it to be a thorn in his pants.

Didn't need me to babysit his children –
did it to keep me near – dangerous toy.

Didn't like his children – disobedient and snarky;
some diluted sense of me, some weight of their father straying.

Didn't love him – didn't like him much: puffy lips, bulged pants,
thick tongue, mostly the tongue.

Bright, demanding teacher, and the thrill of his hand
under my skirt – hidden from my classmates only by his desk.

Driving home from babysitting, he'd park in a lane he knew
was near the home of the science teacher, and although we necked

he was furtive even as he loosed his tongue from behind those
square yellow teeth and pushed it into my mouth,

reminding me of Sunday slabs my grandmother served, hoping I
would eat before discovering the source, the tubefeet like a starfish

Despite occasional headlights, he would uncover my breast, take it
into his mouth full of tongue; would open his pants, put my hand

into his mysterious cave, close it around.
Never saw, had never seen one, being a fatherless, brotherless, girl.

It was only Braille and his heavy breathing and my astonishment
that I could cause this, and all the time, it had nothing to do with him.

Only my cousin – who had once been his favorite, always ahead
of me, showing what could be done if I had her looks, her grades.

After his children were in bed, exploring his desk, I found my cousin's
letters written from college full of eager news, even affection.

But if love letters they dissembled, were coy between the lines.
Then I thought of my eighth grade teacher chastised

and fired for his affair with my classmate. And now, the line
between us and dismissal, shame, civil war.

I was a tease, endless tickle, an ache in the groin.
He was my test case.

And in wanting my body I had him firmly hooked – a fish
always one sharp tug from being lifted from the water.

SLIDE SHOW VII

For when I remember my grandmother with her nimbus of air-white hair, and glasses that flickered with light, sitting by the front window because she could no longer get out and the passing scene below became her life, such a different scene than when she and Henry built the house before the century turned. Then I remember our canasta games, but not exactly when I began to let her win.

Growing Up False or True:
The Unreliable Narrator

Why do you think
I would choose this moment,
and your eager faces to confess
to stealing 34 wallets from the
Five and Dime where they sat
like plastic sheets, so thin,
so poorly made, it was as if
the buyers put them out for kids
to steal, like loss leaders.

Or should I tell you about the man
on the subway, his fingers
palpating from behind, and when I
leaned back against him,
he released his breath in a puff
that stirred the hairs on my neck.

I see you're leaning forward now.
Maybe we should return
to the easy ways to take
a true/false test, involving pencil lead
or eraser, not for answers
but to get away with something,

or when I took Monica's
prissy-pants science project and added
blue dye to the neat little beakers, oh yes,
and just a splash of liquid soap,
not much, so it rambled up the glass sides
and gently flowed over Miss Goody-Penmanship's
careful explanation,

or the times we'd stare at Mr. Vincent's crotch,
you know, everyone at 10:32 – click –
went the clock and we'd stare until
the poor man fumbled toward his zipper,

as did Mr. Ensel with thick fingers
marked with teacher's ink,
when he drove me home
via byway and alley.

And there are more, of course,
many more, but how will you know
if they're true, or not?

Kimble's Pond

I go to Kimble's Pond,
let my feet *crunch* through new snow
blown into freezing
as the red tongue of the thermometer withdraws.

We'd been waiting
for enough cold to snap the last of autumn,
pull remaining leaves from maple and oak.
Now snow has fallen while we slept.

The faint crease of dawn pulls bare tangles
of branches out of the darkness.
Too early for birds, those that are left.

A grey shape looms.
The ice slick that started last week
has filled with weight and reliability.
Night's wind, which blew off the snow's blanket,
swept also leaves and twigs
leaving a blank slate.

There'll be a dark stretch at the far edge
where water spills into a creek. I think
of my cousins, who broke through ice
on another pond, found together
in a frozen embrace.

I take off one glove, clench it in my teeth
and slide my foot into the right skate,
then the left, lace them tight
using my grandmother's button hook.

Lime Kiln Road stretches past like a striped snake.
I am alone at Kimble's Pond with untried ice.

I push off and script my calligraphy
across the surface,
through the center, around the edges

cutting into ice with my crimped toe blades
and listening to the *shooosh* of my tracks,
and I scream out toward the sky.

There's nothing like a pond of your own
as Kimble's was that morning,
like the beginning of the world.
Ice and cold, a sharp cut to the air
working its way to your lungs. It was good
to be first. It never happened again.

No Reunion

We talked of dying today,
old friend, a continent away
near the Sound where we swam
summers into fall. Your husband

too weak to talk, you told me,
suddenly roused himself to correct your grammar.
This is how I'll remember him, correct
and correcting, but you say,
it's all right, this is what you've lived with.

And then you tell me you've been downtown
to find out about Freddie,
beautiful Freddie, with whom I spent passion
and angst from kindergarten's chalky math
to high school beach parties. Freddie's name –
there – on the reunion list of those

who would never attend to see how we've changed,
how we've stayed the same. No one could
add detail to his stark three names
in the list of lost classmates.

You and I battled
our elementary lives over Freddie.
On birthdays in first grade, we got to change desks.
Me next to Freddie in January, usurped by you

in February, and even today, when I call
to wish you Happy Birthday, you gloat again,
and we laugh, but you have bigger news:

Freddie died young. He's been dead for years
and we still carry him as he was when we
first saw, last saw him. Thirty years
he's been alive in our minds – already gone.

Carried him like a fresh baked loaf of bread,
the smell of him, wavy hair, laugh that forced
his head back and to the right. He's kept
those school days near the surface:

dances, spitballs, notes folded impossibly small,
Freddie to Bob to Debbie to me,

covered with graphite and pocket lint, full of
first, sixth grade passion, seventh, tenth.

I never went back to reunion, because
I didn't look the way Freddie remembered me.
And all this time he wasn't there,
couldn't be there, and now I wish
I'd seen him again, hair full or lost,
waist slim or gone, but still,
the familiar dint in his chin.

Chestnut Tree on Forest Street

The last time I climbed the tree
I didn't know I would outgrow
its long horizontal limbs
branched like a cradle, didn't know
the need to be in a tree would be forgotten,
how rough bark against my legs
was like conversation. Places my fingers tucked into
held safety like the mahogany banister
leading to the second floor.
I didn't worry about what lived in crevices
only that my fingers fit, and the tree held.
I winched my way higher, higher,
until the sky seemed closer than the ground
and truer.

About CB Follett

CB Follett was the winner of the 2001 National Poetry Book Award from Salmon Run Press for her book AT THE TURNING OF THE LIGHT. She has been nominated for numerous Pushcart Prizes, including twice as a poet and been a prize winner in the Ann Stanford Prize, Northwoods Journal Poetry Prize, New Press Literary Quarterly poetry contest, Portland Festival Prize, Robert Winner Award, the George Bogin Award, Billee Murray Denny Prize, The Climbing Art, and finalist in the Agnes Fay Di Castignola Award, among others. She is the recipient of a grant for poetry from the Marin Arts Council. This is her sixth poetry collection. She was publisher and co-editor of RUNES, A Review of Poetry. CB Follett lives with her husband in Sausalito, California, perched on a hill between the coastal range and San Francisco Bay.